Forging Made Easy

How To Get Started In Forging, Blacksmithing And Bladesmithing As A Complete Beginner (Including Creative Projects To Get Started)

CW01432687

Introduction

Twenty years later, Dean Harvey still has a spark in his eyes when talking about what he does best: bladesmithing. He began hand-forging blades in 1986 and received his Master smith rating in 1992.

In 2004, his career began elevating him to new heights because Dean was offered a position on the American Society Board. If this elevation is not enough, Dean later served as vice-president of the Texas Knifemakers and Collectors Associations.

For his rate card, he says he sells $450 for hunters and $700 for bowies, and many of his knives have been featured in many magazines and global publications.

Today, blade and blacksmithing do not get the recognition it deserves, while the truth is, what you can do as a blade and blacksmith today is vast. You can make many pieces in addition to making blades. For example, you can create custom craft wrenches, dies and jigs, shovels, bicycle stands, fences, shoe horses, home décor items, and creative decorative iron pieces. You can also take your career a note higher and become a historical educator!

As for making money as a blade and blacksmith, this career path has great monetary prospects. According to The American Farrier's Journal, a part-time farrier can make as much as $20,000 yearly![1] This means you can make much more if you do it as a full-time job, especially if you continuously enhance your skills.

Are you a blade and blacksmith die-hard fan who would like to venture into this art but are hesitant because you are unsure how to go about it?

Have you have been looking for a book that has the basics you need to kickstart your career and illustrated projects and variations you can get into right away?

If so, then you are in the right place!

Here is a preview of what you will learn from this book:

- A better understanding of what blade and blacksmithing is

- Essential tools you will need to get started

---

[1] https://www.americanfarriers.com/articles/12137-full-time-farrier-income-skyrockets?v=preview

- Detailed beginner blade and blacksmithing projects, with each having a simple-to-understand step-by-step illustration

- How to polish and maintain the completed projects

- **And much more!**

As you start reading this book, you will learn that blade and blacksmithing are not as challenging as you may have thought!

Get comfortable and walk with me on this journey

Let us get started.

PS: I'd like your feedback. If you are happy with this book, please leave a review on Amazon.

Please leave a review for this book on Amazon by visiting the page below:

https://amzn.to/2VMR5qr

Table of Contents

Forging Made Easy

Chapter 1: Forging 101

As a blacksmith, you will have a lot of freedom on what you can make. Tom Peterson, for example, a Montana Farrier, captured the World Championship Blacksmiths Title by making a horseshoe in 2019.

Lisa Thompson, owner of The Farrier's Wife Blacksmith Shop[2] in Ste. Genevieve, Missouri, has a home forge she uses to create custom works of steel like decorative garden ornaments, commissioned pieces, letter openers, and hooks.

As you can see, being both a black and bladesmith is interesting and provides lots of room for imagination.

That aside, let us now look at what really blacksmithing and bladesmithing are and what the difference between the two is:

Understanding Blacksmithing and Bladesmithing

Also known as smiths or craftsmen, blacksmiths are artists who use iron to fabricate objects through hot and/or cold forging, normally done on an anvil. (An anvil is a solid block

---

[2] https://www.facebook.com/TheFarriersWifeBlacksmithShop/

of metal or what is known as cast steel and always has a flat top surface).

On the other hand, bladesmithing is an art. Through this art, bladesmiths make knives, blades, and swords, using tools such as hammer, forge, anvil, just to mention a few.

Bladesmithing also involves employing relevant techniques similar to those used in blacksmithing and woodworking that help forgers create custom swords and knife sword handles. Finally, bladesmithing incorporates leatherworking. Leatherworking is important because it helps in the making of sheathes.

With what we have mentioned so far, we can agree that the two are somehow different. How? Allow me to elaborate.

The first thing to note is that bladesmithing is part of blacksmithing, which means that blacksmithing revolves around forging steel while blade smithing revolves around making blades like knives and daggers, just to mention a few.

There are several tools you can forge as a blacksmith. They include:

- **Armor:** Metal plate suits, helmets, chain mail shirts, and many more

- **Hardware pieces**: Hinges, screws, bolts, brackets, hooks, handles, locks, keys, and many more

- **Tools**: Crowbars, hammers, shovels, vices, axes, and many more

- **Decorative objects:** Candlesticks, hanging artwork, sculptures, indoor and outdoor garden trellises, and many more

- **Household items:** Cooking utensils, light fixtures, railings, furniture, home fittings, for example, fireplace fittings, and many more

- **Religious Artifacts:** Crosses, patens, chalices, tabernacles, credence tables, and many more.

- **Jewelry:** Earrings, necklaces, watches, rings, and many more.

- **Structural tools:** Fences, gates, balconies, grills, windows, and many more

- **Agricultural tools:** Horse shoes and nails, plowshares, sickles, cowbells, and many more

- **Musical instruments:** Steel drums, bells, cymbals, gongs, chimes, and many more

- **And items such as** spikes, boot scrapers, tents, stakes, and many more!

For bladesmiths, things might seem less interesting since all you think you will be doing is make knives, right?

WRONG!

Take the example of making knives. With techniques learned from this book, you can make custom and unique:

- Pocket knives

- Boning knives

- Sashimi bōchō

- Bowie knives

- Machetes

- Mezzaluna

- Yanagi ba

- Grapefruit knives

- Butcher knives

- Deba bōchō

- And many more knives!

As we have just seen, there are no limits to what you can design and create with knives, and this is just an example of what you can do as a bladesmith. The thing is, bladesmithing is vast because it also involves making daggers and swords.

Making swords may seem like a thing of the past, but designing and forging swords can also be lucrative for you.

Look at a company like Purpleheart Armoury,[3] an active company in the HEMA, Mixed Weapons Martial Arts, SCA, WMA, and FMA, to mention a few known for their sword collections. These companies show that bladesmithing can also be a career that fills you with pride and joy.

To start us off on the journey to becoming a master forger, you need to get your tools ready. In the next chapter, we will discuss the tools you need to have in your workshop.

---

[3] https://www.woodenswords.com/default.asp

Chapter 2: The Forger's Toolbox – Blacksmith's Tools

If you Google "blacksmith tools," the search results will show you a whole bunch of tools. Although most of these tools have a place in your workshop, you do not need all of them to get started.

The following are the most vital globally recognized tools needed for your blacksmithing needs:

A forge

A blacksmithing forge is a type of hearth used to heat and shape metals into desired objects. Simply put, a forge is an open furnace where metal ore and metal are heated.

A forge works almost like a wood-burning stove, but in this case, the heat source varies as most forges use coal and others use solar power or gas.

Gas forges

This type of forge is the best for beginners. It is the easiest to use because the fire produced is consistent, clean, and easy to control.

Also, gas forges save time that you could otherwise spend on getting the forge ready for days in order to have it warmed up enough to working temperature. Also, after some practice, you will realize that you will produce more forged items than a smith who uses coal forges.

Using this type of forge is also very beneficial, health-wise. For example, working on a project using an open pan forge for a whole weekend can cause health complications because of breathing in excessive coal.[4] Also, if your workshop is closer to neighbors, using gas forges is the best way to go —it

---

[4]   https://earthjustice.org/sites/default/files/files/coal-ash-man_COMPLETE_2017-07-20_light.pdf

is unlikely that your neighbor will like the acrid coal smoke drifting in through their open windows.

Gas is also more accessible than coal. Eia: U.S Energy Information Administration says that the top coal-producing state is Wyoming which produced 41 percent only.[5] This means to access coal, you will have to make planned trips while for gas, you would not need to go through the same.

Also, many mines are closing mostly because of the tough Federal regulation like the *Federal Coal Mine Health and Safety Act of 1969* controlling the management of coal mines, making coal accessibility even more difficult.

NOTE: There is something that I would like to make clear about gas forges:

You might come across information that gas forges cannot forge weld. This is not entirely true but can happen if you don't have a properly designed forge. If you get a gas forge properly equipped with a designed burner that is big and equipped with enough burners, you will never have a problem forging a weld.

There are two types of highly-recommended gas forges:

---

[5] https://www.eia.gov/energyexplained/coal/where-our-coal-comes-from.php

- Propane forge double burner unit
- Portable propane forge single burner knife and tool making farrier forge

Induction Forges

This type of forge uses an induction coil to heat metal. The forge's heating system preheats the metal and presses it into shape using a press or a hammer.

If you decide to use induction forging, you will learn that the whole forging process is controllable. You see, heating systems such as gas furnaces require a preheat and a shutdown but with induction forging, you do not have to worry about this because the process is highly calculated.

Induction forging also saves a lot of energy. The heat from the forge is available whenever you need it. For example, if an interruption ever occurs downstream, you can turn the power off, thus preventing any unnecessary energy loss.

The energy-saving also comes from how heat is generated: within the component, not around it. That energy generation technology makes energy and heat transfer more efficient mainly because the workpiece is the only thing that receives the heating from the induction heating system, which means that the atmosphere surrounding the workpiece will not be affected.

Global warming is becoming a factor to consider; induction forging helps conserve the environment. You see, induction forging does not produce any harmful byproducts (smoke or toxins) during the process.

The induction forge has different power supplies, ranging from 50Hz to 200kHz, which is higher than typical household electrical power. You will probably need to set up a new circuit or install a new transformer to accommodate this forge.

Solid Fuel Forges

This type of forge uses various kinds of fuel:

- Lump coal

- Charcoal briquettes

- Wood (soft and hard wood)

- Coal (For coal, go for either Lignite Bituminous or anthracite because they provide sufficient heat)

- Coke

The coal forge is large and has a better open-hearth pan, thus giving you more room for working with larger or more oddly shaped pieces. With this type of forge, it is easier to find the right position to heat your metal, and you will often get the required results. If you decide to get quicker results, you can choose charcoal, but you can go for coal if you intend to work on a project that requires average heat.

Blacksmith's Vise

This tool helps hold hot iron firmly during hammering, twisting, or chiseling.

Hammers

No blacksmith can underrate the place of a hammer in their forge. Hammers act as an extension of your arm, and with them, your unique pieces will come to life!

Just as we have seen with forges, you will find a wide variety of blacksmithing hammers in the market. What to note is that not all the hammers you buy will serve the same purpose in your workshop.

Thus, choosing the right hammer will not be easy as a beginner, and that is why I will show you the types of hammers you should have now as a beginner and the ones you should buy once you become a pro. Before we get into the type of hammer you should have, there are a few considerations to keep in mind:

Style and type of hammer

When purchasing a hammer, you should find out what type it is and its purpose. You can try answering the following questions to guide you:

Do I intend to make a decorative piece?

Do I intend to venture into farrier work?

Most hammers have two ends, also known as faces, which come in different shapes. When deciding which hammer to buy, it is important to focus more on the core type than the style. What does this mean?

Well, hammers are similar in design but are somehow still different. These tiny differences are apparent when looking at the overall style of the hammer you intend to purchase. In most cases, style indicates the country of origin and from these countries. For example, some hammers have New England, Japanese, and Swedish styles.

Consider the following picture of the Swedish Ball Peen Hammer, for example;

For this hammer, the type is "cross peen," and the style is "Swedish." To know which style is best, go for what feels comfortable and economical for the piece you are about to forge. As a beginner, the best hammer is what fits and works in your hand.

The hammer's weight and usability properties

Depending on your strength and skill, you will find that hammers have different weights. However, if you want to flatten or remove huge amounts of material, you will need to rely on your skill more than the hammer's weight.

In most cases, if you think about weight, you should consider an example like forming hot metal within a range of one to 3 inches in diameter. Some smiths can do this with heavy hammers, but you should know that you can also do it with a light hammer!

Here is the bottom line:

A light hammer will be easier to handle, but you should know that the same hammer will not help you achieve what you desire in most cases because it has a lower driving force than what heavy hammers produce. That does not mean light hammers are useless in forging. Light hammers will allow you to hone your hammering skills so that when you wield a heavy hammer, you produce better pieces.

Wooden or Broke hammers

I recommend hammers made with wooden grips. Some will suggest fiberglass or plastic grips, but these materials do not fit well with smiths' workshops because of the heat produced by the forge.

Wooden grips offer protection against heat and tend to be quite comfortable when working for long durations. In addition to the material of the grip, go for hammers with the length you prefer. By handling different hammers with different lengths, you will know the perfect length for you.

With these considerations in mind, the following are the common blacksmith's hammers available:

Blacksmith Ball Peen (Pein) Hammer

Blacksmith Cross Peen (Pein) Hammer

Blacksmith Rounding Hammer

Chasing hammer

Forming hammer

Forging Made Easy

<u>*Goldsmith's hammer*</u>

<u>*Planishing Hammer*</u>

Riveting hammer

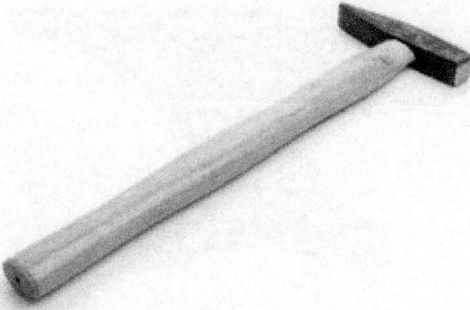

Wood Mallet

Anvil

As mentioned earlier, an anvil is a wrought or cast iron construct used to flatten metal with a hammer. An anvil will have the following parts:

The face

This is the flat surface on top of the structure. You will use this top surface to strike your metal workpieces. Therefore, this is the part of the anvil that you will mostly use.

Even though this part of the anvil will rarely get directly hit by the hammer, you should ensure that the face material can withstand any heavy blow without losing its shape or breaking.

The horn

This is the cone-like part of the anvil that is typically in front of the anvil. The main use of this part is bending your metal, and it usually does not have to be made of the same hard material as the surface of the anvil.

The table of the anvil

Also referred to as the step, the anvil's table is a narrow flat surface part of the anvil located between the face and the horn part. The table's height is higher than the horn and is lower than the anvil's face. Refrain from using this part to cut workpieces on its edge because you can cause wear to its features. Rather, use other metal-cutting tools.

The Hardie hole

You will find this part of the anvil inside the face's surface on the end opposite of the heel —also known as the horn. If you look closely at this part, you might liken it to a square-shaped mouth.

You use this to hold rod-like tools such as swages and chisels. Also, this part of the anvil is useful for bending metal and punching forgings.

The pritchel hole

This hole is similar to the hardy hole. You will find it located a short distance from the hole inside the face's surface. The difference lies in its mouth since its circular, which you will use to punch holes that are rounded into a workpiece.

Considerations before buying an anvil

Anvils might seem easy to purchase because of their simple features. However, the truth is that purchasing anvils is something you should do with a lot of careful consideration to ensure what you buy meets your needs.

As you go anvil shopping, consider the following factors:

The material

History tells us that anvils were made with bronze, stone, and wrought iron. Nowadays, steel is considered the best material. Steel is the preferred material due to its favorable properties and easy accessibility since it is mass-produced.

However, we still have anvils made with cast iron. Please note that cast iron anvils have less face rebound (face rebound is how the hardness of the face functions) and are more brittle.

Overall, note that hard metals have greater face rebound, which means you should consider such materials for the anvil. Forged steel anvils are also effective, but many smiths go for wrought and cast-iron anvils with welded steel faces on the top.

Its work and forging intentions

Before you buy an anvil, think of how you will use it. For example, if you will pursue black and bladesmithing as a hobby, it will be unnecessary to purchase large and highly-expensive anvils. Also, it is important to assess if you can use the anvil you intend to purchase in more than one way. If its applications can overlap with those of other anvils, the better it is.

Its shape, weight, and size

If you want the perfect anvil for your workshop, you should consider these three factors. The size, for example, predicts what you can use the anvil for.

Here, worth noting is that the heavier your anvil, the easier time you will have using it.

Its cost

What we have discussed as considerations so far impacts the price of anvils. For example, you might find small anvils going for between $2 and $5 per pound, while bigger ones might go for around $7 and $9 per pound. Also, consider the shipping cost because the heavier your anvil will be, the more you will have to pay.

With the considerations in mind, the following are some of the best anvils in the market so far:

Hardy Tools

Also known as bottom or anvil tools, hardy tools are metalworking tools. You use these metalworking tools with your anvil. There are several types of hardy tools available:

- Cut-offs hardy tools

- Bending hardy tools

- Shaping or forming hardy tools

Chisel

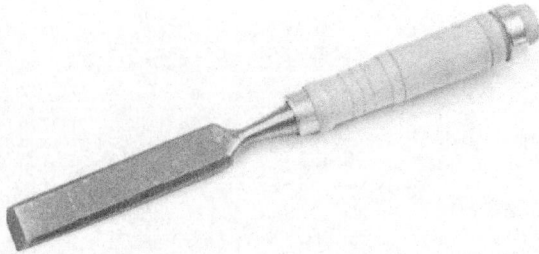

The chisel's end enables you to cut metal, and its wooden or metallic grip helps you work with both hot and cold metal.

There are several types of chisels. The most common ones are:

Cold chisels

This chisel is made of steel that goes through several shifts of hardening, making it very durable. The durability and strength of this chisel make it ideal for cutting any material that is softer than this tool. It can sufficiently cut off rusted bolts and rivets.

Cape Chisels

This type of chisel has a long, tapered blade, making it perfect for creating unique details and art on metals by curving tiny grooves into the surface. This chisel is from the cold chisel family, but it has an added special look.

Gouge chisels

This chisel type has a curved blade that resembles a half-moon. It is essential for cutting round or semi-circular grooves in metal.

Power chisels

Since we live in the technological era, you should consider having power chisels in your workshop. These chisels are powered by a motor that gives them more power and helps with accuracy —at least compared to hand chisels.

Tongs

Having a tool you can use to strike the metal is not enough; you also need something to help you hold the said piece. That is where tongs come into play to make your work easier. However, you need to get the right tongs.

Choosing the wrong tongs can be dangerous. Wrong tongs can lead to self-injuries as the tongs can slip and fall on your legs.

I remember an instance where I was trying to hold a thick round bar with some small tongs. This incident did not end well because the hot bar slipped and hit my arm. Trust me, the evidence of that mistake is still visible to date. I cannot stress enough how important it is to buy the right tongs.

Tongs generally have three primary parts:

- **Handles:** Also called the reins, this part of your tongs helps you handle them (its purpose is simple, as the name suggests). As a beginner, you should not go for heavy tongs unless you consider it necessary.

- **Joints**: This part of the tongs allows you to open and close the tongs.

- **Jaws**: This part helps with gripping, and it is the one that is in direct contact with the hot forge and metal.

The length of your tongs should range anywhere between 16 and 22 inches, but generally, tongs range between 10 to 40 inches. Note that the longer the tongs, the heavier they will be. The benefit of having long tongs is that you will be further away from the hot forge. All in all, the length depends on the specific project you are working on.

The following are the most common types of blacksmithing tongs;

- **Flat-jaw tongs:** These are perfect for flat materials, thanks to their flat jaws. You can also use them to hold the stock if your tongs have tongs in the middle.

- **V-bit Tongs:** These tongs have a letter v shape, allowing you to grip your pieces more tightly. You can also use the v-tongs to hold flat stock, but you should preferably use them more to hold square and round stock.

- **Wolf-jaw Tongs**: These tongs are perfect for general purposes. Their 'teeth' hold all kinds of stocks, making this tong beginner and expert friendly. All the shapes you will find of wolf-jaw tongs hold round, flat, and square stock securely.

- **Pickup tongs:** As the name suggests, we use these tongs for picking things up. From time to time, you will notice some pieces near the forge or on the floor, and using your bare hands is not recommended, making pickup tongs very handy.

- **Bolt-jaw Tongs:** These tongs have a curved opening that allows you to pass bolts and other pieces that have odd shapes. For example, if you will make an s-hook, you should have bolt-jaw tongs in your workshop.

- **Box-jaw tongs:** These tongs are an improved version of flat-jaw tongs. The only difference is that box-jaw tongs have box-like jaws with two lips on each side. You need these tongs in your workshop because they will come in handy when you need to keep metal from sliding off.

As we have seen, there are several types of tongs. The question now is, *which are the best tongs for beginners?*

The rule of thumb is to go for wolf-jaw tongs because they hold all sorts of different shapes and sizes of materials. Wolf-jaw tongs are also easily accessible and are economically friendly. Therefore, go for two different sizes of wolf-jaw tongs.

Punch

As the name suggests, we use a punch to punch a hole in metal; it is also handy when putting a decorative stamp on your metal.

Swage

This is a heavy block of steel or cast iron (it comes in different sized shapes and holes and mostly with forms on the sides) that you will use to hold, support, or back up a hot bar of metal for better shaping.

Chapter 3: The Forger's Toolbox – Bladesmith Tools

There is a huge overlap between the tools you will use while blacksmithing and bladesmithing. Although the tools serve similar functions, some specialized tools will enable you to accomplish specific tasks in bladesmithing, just like we have seen while discussing blacksmithing tools.

Bladesmithing and blacksmithing have these tools in common:

- Forge

- Anvils

- Tongs

- Punches

The following are tools specifically suited for bladesmithing:

Grinders

Grinders help smoothen out the surface of the blade. They also help remove the excess metal on the blades. To help save time and energy, go for an electric grinder.

Electric saws

With the help of electric saws, you can remove excess metal from your starting materials to attain the needed blade size for your projects.

Pyrometers

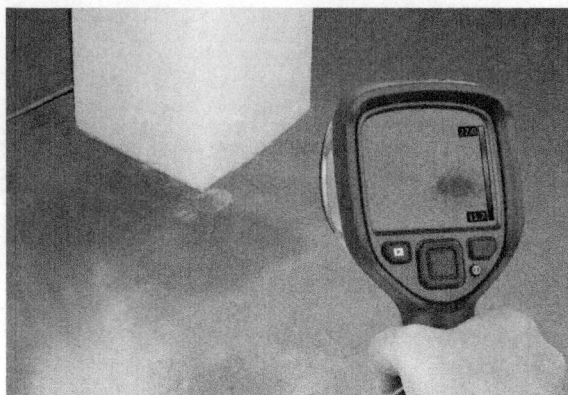

This tool can also work with blacksmithing.

As a forger, you need to determine how close you are to the ideal working temperature. Sometimes, a blade can be too hot to handle or too cold, which tends to be unfavorable, making it important to invest in a pyrometer to help you measure the blade's temperature.

Swages and Drifts

This tool is similar to the blacksmith's punch; the key difference is that you use it to expand the hole created by the punch. Swages and drifts come in different sizes and face diameters, making it important to choose one that favors your projects. With this tool, the process of bending the blade becomes easier.

Sandpaper

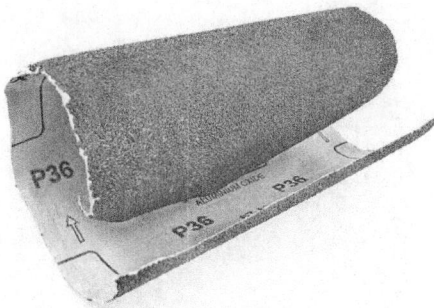

Your blades will need finishing, which is where sandpaper comes in. Through its rough, textured surface, you will smooth out the blade's imperfections and level the blade's surface.

You will find two types of sandpapers in the market; wet and dry sandpapers. Wet sandpapers are best after completing your project because they are less abrasive than dry sandpapers. On the other hand, dry sandpapers are best for removing imperfections and smoothening rough material quickly and easily.

There are more general tools you should have. They are:

Heat-resistant aprons

With this apron, you will protect yourself from the heat, which can otherwise make black and bladesmithing challenging. Also, some aprons come with practical compartments where you can store the essential tools you need for the project you are working on.

Heat Resistant Gloves

Since you will be working with hot materials, you need to ensure you have a pair or two of these gloves. These gloves will allow you to pick objects without much risk of burns and other injuries.

Forging Made Easy

Safety Glasses

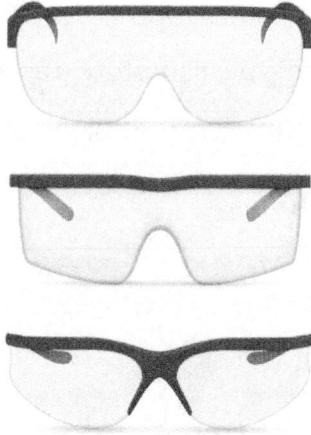

These glasses will help protect you from eye injuries.

Masks

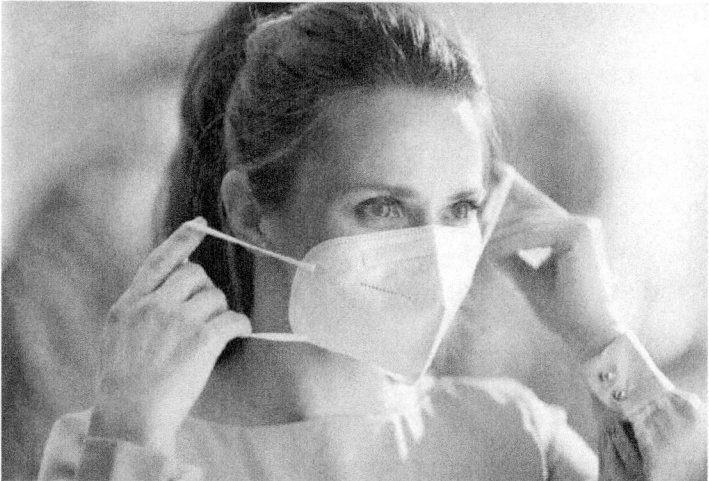

Earplugs and muffs

Safety Boots

Quenching Oil

Blade and blacksmithing have a process called quenching that involves placing or dipping the heated metal in quenching oil to control and limit the metal's cooling microstructure effects.

Magnets

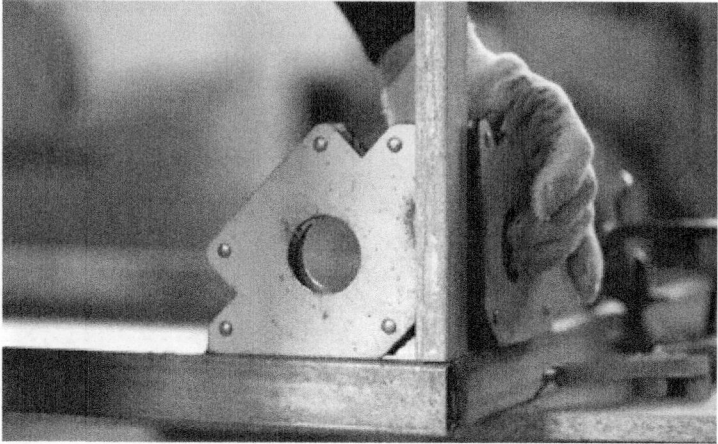

Magnets help gauge the temperature of the blade. It is crucial to know how high or low the magnet's temperature is because if you let your material get too hot, it can cause warps, and in other cases, it causes the metal to crack.

Belt Sander

This tool is important for sharpening and forging knives.

Steel Rulers

This ruler will come in handy when measuring actual sizes in metric or imperial measurements. You will also use it for drawing straight lines.

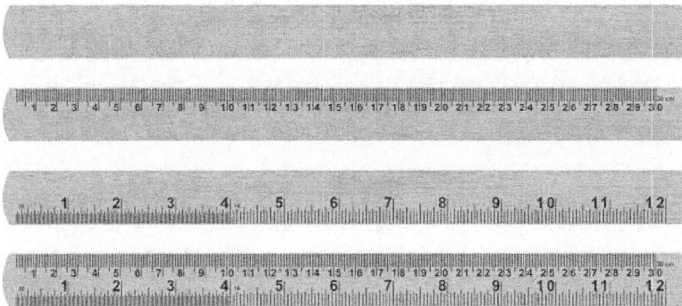

With all these tools in your workshop, you are now ready to begin working on your projects. However, before you begin, there are a few things to consider. Let us discuss this further in the next chapter.

Chapter 4: What to Note Before Getting into Blade and Blacksmithing

Every task usually has challenges; the same applies to blade and blacksmithing. Hence, you need to be aware of a couple of things as you get started.

Mental and Physical fitness

Sometimes, your projects will not be as you had initially planned, and other times, you might have a hard time doing something like punching as best as you can, which can be very demoralizing.

Therefore, ensure you are both psychologically and mentally fit all through your forging career by:

- Always think outside the box. Even when projects are not going according to plan, learn how to problem-solve to have the project fit the pre-set needs.

- Always be patient. You see, being a smith requires you to have solid hand-eye coordination, strength, and cognitive skills. You need the virtue of patience to get the results you want. With the skills you will gain over time, you will get better.

- To become the black and bladesmith you desire to be, you need to have a substantial amount of stamina and mastery over the art of applying the right amount of force at the right spot to deform the metal as required. In addition, you need to have the right tools and the right setup that will help you work for long periods.

Get tools

Having personal tools will allow you to practice at your own pace and whenever you want.

Even when I was an apprentice in someone else's shop, I still needed to do more practice because there were times when I needed to recreate some of the projects I had learned earlier.

Get a workspace

Like getting tools, getting a workspace is another important factor to consider before you begin the actual blade and blacksmithing. It is in your best interest to have a place where you can practice by yourself while still learning and a place where you can store your tools.

On average, if you could get a 12 by 14-foot dimension space, you will be set to begin your forger's career. However, remember that as you mature in this career, you will need more tools, hence a bigger workspace.

Always mind your safety

You can take many steps to ensure you remain as safe as possible while working in your workshop. Let us mention a few of these steps:

- **Never forget to use your protective accessories while working**: Remember to always wear your apron and safety glasses while in your workshop because hot sparks and flashes are unavoidable. It is also important to have your mask on during forging to keep off fine ash and black soot from your sinus airways. The loud hammering can also damage your hearing, which is why you need to have your earplugs on.

- **Ensure your workshop has proper ventilation:** Burning fuel generates carbon monoxide, which, as you know, is poisonous. Ensuring your workshop is properly ventilated will ensure that air sufficiently circulates within your working space.

- **Be attentive to your well-being:** You might be having an overflow of projects in your mind, and in as much as you will have the urge to finish them all as fast as possible, please remember that you are not a robot. You need adequate rest to function at an optimal level. Do not work when you feel dizzy, tired, hungry, high, or sick, to mention a few.

- **Invest in a first aid kit:** Your career in forging will come with minor and major cuts, scratches, and burns, no matter how careful you try to be. Therefore, have a fully equipped blacksmith's first aid kit. This kit will serve as your first response in the event of an accident.

- **Use functional tools only:** Having functional tools in your workshop is vital because you will get the best results, all while being safe. Go out of your way to avoid using malfunctioned or damaged tools.

- **Treat all metal as hot:** Metal might be in its original color and still be hot. Just because metal is not orange and red does not mean it is not hot. To minimize confusion and injuries, find some specific space in your shop where you will be placing your hot pieces. This way, you will minimize the chances of getting burned.

Everything we have discussed in the last few chapters has sufficiently prepared you for the next part of the book: hands-on projects with step-by-step instructions:

Chapter 5: 25 Black and Blade Smithing Projects With Step-by-Step Instructions

This section will walk you through easy black and bladesmithing projects that will empower you to create more projects.

Project 1: Forged Coat Hook

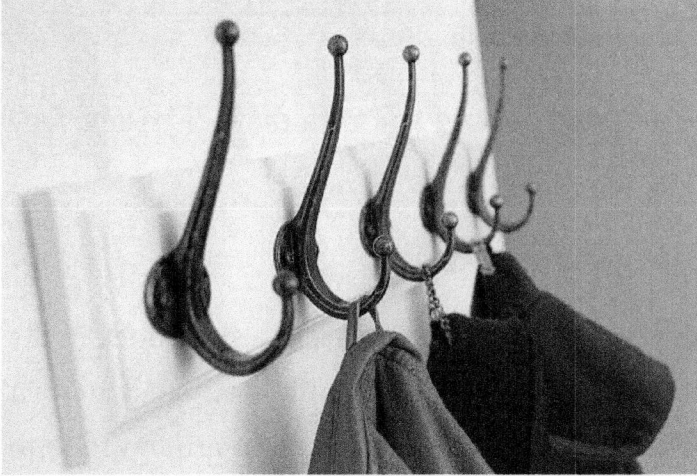

For this project, you will need the following tools;

- Tongs

- Metal Stock

- Anvil

- Forge

- Hammer (Flat faced)

- Punch

- Vise

- Twisting wrench

- Metal wire brush

With your safety gear on and with the tools ready, follow the following steps;

Step 1: Shoulder creation

With the help of your tongs, place the steel stock in the forge and remove it when orange. For the steel stock to turn to an orange heat, the temperature should be around 1600 to 1800 degrees F.

Place your orange steel stock above the edge (preferable 10 degrees looking towards the downwards angle) and strike at the edge of the anvil. The aim of doing this is to create a shoulder.

Then, bring your piece to level and strike the steel stock until it flattens to a piece measuring 3/16 inches (your hammering technique should be in a way that works on the edges consistently).

Step 2: Punch a hole

Once you have created the shoulder, punch your steel stock consistently and only stop when you get three quarters through. Reposition the anvil, then center the steel stock on the anvil. Again, punch the stock until you get three quarters through.

Now punch a hole on the plate and drive the punch into the hole until you knock out the plug. Finally, cool the punch tool and return your stock into the forge (ensure you enter the square end first).

Step 3: Forming the hook scroll

Get your stock out and place it at the edge of the anvil. With angled blows, swing blows to the edge of the bar, making sure to turn 90 degrees after each swing until you taper the tip to 1/16 inches. Then, lie your stock flat and strike the top of the taper (ensure you turn 90 degrees after each hit. Also, rotate 180 degrees after every seven hits).

Pick your tongs and work on the stock lightly until your taper is 3/8 of an inch to 1/16 of an inch over three inches. Then, pick your piece from the forge (shoulder up) and place it on your anvil (the piece should be around a half-inch over the edge of the anvil). While on top of the anvil, strike lightly past the edge until bent into an 'L' shape. Finally, rotate the tip of the stock and strike the tip towards you until you form a scroll, then quench the scroll.

Step 4: Making small scrolls close to the point

With your quenched piece, place the stock on the anvil horn, ensuring the scroll faces up, with a half-inch of the piece hanging off the horn. With your hammer, strike a small scroll until the taper bends downwards. Stretch out another half-inch of the piece and strike it again until you get an 'L' shape.

Take the piece, rotate it 180 degrees, and place it on the anvil (the small scroll you made should be facing up). Then, using your hammer, strike the small scroll towards you. Finally, when the backing plate is on the forge table, place the hook on the forge.

Step 5: Twisting the center

Take the hook off the forge after it hits full heat and place it in the vise (the small scroll should be at the top of the vise jaws). Once adequately supported by the vise, pull up the twisting wrench and twist with one turn.

Step six: Finishing up

With the center twisted, return your hook into the forge, then using a metal brush, scrape off the slag formed due to the repeated heating. After removing the slag, dip your hook in a bucket of oil and cover it completely. Finally, hold your piece against the forge until the color turns matte black.

Project 2: Forged Sword

This project is easy but dangerous, and it is up to you to decide how sharp you want your sword to be. Also, before you begin working on this project, decide if you will want to make an ornamental sword for hanging on walls or whether the said sword will have a more functional value.

For this project, you will need:

- Anvil

- Hammer

- Vise

- Tongs

- Forge

- Damascus steel or any High Carbon steel

- Sandpaper

- Magnet

- Quenching oil

- Belt sander

With your tools ready, follow along to make this piece:

Forging Made Easy

Step 1: Design your sword

You can choose from several designs, and it is important to start with a simple design. Research traditional swords to get inspiration on which design to settle on. From there, draw out the design on paper and start your project with stock steel. Make sure the stock is approximately the length of your final design.

Step 2: Heat your stock until yellow

Using a pair of tongs, heat your stock in your forge until it changes color to yellow —which means the temperature should be around 2,000 degrees Fahrenheit.

Step 3: Shape the stock

After heating the stock to the appropriate temperature, remove it from the forge and set it on the anvil. Use a hammer to shape the corner of the stock into the shape of the sword you would like. Keep in mind that you need to taper both sides of the steel evenly.

Step 4: Flatten your sword's blade

The next step will be to create that cutting edge on both sides of the sword. To do this, you will have to bevel the edges of the steel. After hammering one side, flip the sword on the anvil and repeat the same with the other side.

Step 5: Heat and cool

Once done with the shape, put the sword back in the forge and reheat it to normalize the steel. With your tongs, grip the steel and ensure it is at a non-magnetic temperature of around 1,420 degrees Fahrenheit. Once you have the sword heated up to that temperature, allow the sword to cool off at room temperature. Once the sword is free of the red color, return it to the forge and redo this step three more times.

Step 6: Sand your blade

Once the sword is at room temperature, sand it using the belt sander or by hand to smooth out the edges.

Step 7: Sharpen and strengthen your blade

By this time, your sword is beveled, normalized, and sanded (by now, you can see your design come to life). The next important thing to do is reheat the sword and dip it in oil until it reaches room temperature (quenching). The trick is to make sure you transfer the blade from the fire to the quenching oil as fast as you possibly can because if you do not do this, your blade will not harden as it should.

Step 8: Reheat

Regulate your forge to a low temperature and reheat the quenched sword in your forge. The reheating will relax the stress and brittle state brought about by the quenching process.

Step 9: Create the hilt

With your sword almost ready, it is time to create your blade's handle. In this project, let us make a wooden handle.

The first step you should take is to wrap around three layers of tape around the blade part of your knife or sword. To help you do this, you can use masking tape, duct tape, or electrical tape. Remember to wrap the tape from the tip of the knife down to the base where your blade ends, but do not cover the blade's tang.

Next, find two pieces of wood that will comfortably cover the knife's scales. For example, if your project was a normal kitchen knife, you will need to find two 0.64cm pieces of wood. The secret is to ensure that the wood is a little larger than the tang. For your blade to have that desired finish, make sure the grain runs along the length of the wood. The best woods to work with is ash, bois d'arc, pecan, pear, peach, and apple.

If you had purchased a knife kit, you would realize that you have already-cut knife pins. If you do not have a knife kit, you will need to cut it yourself by cutting the metal rods (you will need to set the rod down on a stable surface and use a metal saw or a file to cut into the lengths you desire).

You should note that the rods you will need depend on how many holes you put in the tang. Most blades have two holes, but others have four holes. Once you get your pins ready, file the ends down with a grinder — if you did not purchase a knife kit.

Next, line your vise with plywood and plastic wrap. Only do this step when you are ready to glue everything together. For the glue, you can use epoxy glue because it sets everything much quicker. Simply put, you will need to attach a piece of plywood to each side of your vise and fold a sheet of plastic wrap and tuck it between the vises.

With all this set, it is time to drill the pinholes. For this, you will need to tape the scales and tang together by setting the tang on top, then wrapping a piece of masking tape around the middle to ensure you have everything held together.

Next, use your drill to make the holes. Remember to use the tang's holes as a guide. After making the holes, insert the pins we made earlier in the holes and when completely done, remove the tape and trace the tang onto the scales.

After removing the tang, cut the scales using a band saw or a scroll. Next, sand and polish the top edge of the scales as desired —it is best to do this step now because it will not be possible after you assemble the knife handle, especially at the top-narrow edge of the knife that touches the base of the blade.

Next, ensure the tang on both sides of the blade is clean, then glue the scales together —Gluing will need you to prepare the epoxy glue then apply it to the tang. Then, insert your handle into your vise and clamp it shut. To avoid excess epoxy from spilling off, ensure you place the handles between the pieces of the plastic wrap. Let the epoxy sit for around one hour before moving on to the next step.

https://www.pexels.com/photo/crop-craftsman-with-orbital-sander-5710743/

To finish the handle, grind off any excess pins, if any, and carve the handle with a belt sander. Ensure you sand until you reach the metal part of the tang. Finally, remove the tape from the blade.

Step 10: Sharpen the blade

With your blade done and the handle made, fine file and whetstone your blade carefully until satisfied.

Project 3: Forged Fork

For this project, you will need;

- Tongs

- Ball Peen Hammer

- Forge

- Vise

- Anvil

- Steel Stock

- Metal Wire Brush

- Punch

- Plasma cutting torch

Step 1: Tapering of the fork handle

Mark one end of your bar (quarter-inch by a half-inch, four to six inches long) using a center punch (You need to do this in two spots: two inches from the edge and on the very edge.)

Next, using your tongs, place the end into the forge (with the tongs, hold your stock piece at the taper angle) and then proceed to use angled blows to swing until the tip of the stock is 3/16 of the inch. From the center punch, taper to one inch while ensuring the thickness remains at a quarter inch.

Step 2: Shape the neck

Ensure the anvil horn matches the hammer radius when placing the stock on the anvil, which means it should be halfway between the center punch and the end of the taper.

Next, place the neck of the horn and forge the stock to less than half an inch on the wide side and ensure that the shape flattens to a thickness size of a quarter inch (you will be able to comfortably do this if you use the anvil horn and the anvil face for tapering). To complete the shaping, flatten all faces using the flat-faced hammer.

Step 3: Hot cutting the prongs

Place the piece center punch face up and line up the flat-edged hot cut with the center punch marks. Next, hit the hot cut to mark and strike until cut through. Finally, flip the piece and cut it at the union. You can use the plasma cutting torch for this process too.

Step 4: Tapering the prongs

Strike one of the prongs until you get a 90-degree bend, rotate it at an angle of 180 degrees, and bend it back to half an inch from the face of your anvil. Next, square, then taper the edges from an eighth to 3/16 of one inch.

After finishing the length, mark it from the edge of the anvil to the hardy. With an octagon then round motion, work on the edges of your piece and mark the finished length.

Reheat the finished piece in the forge. Then, bend the fork prong out of your way to move the flat piece so that it can taper. Next, taper the piece from 3/8 to 1/16 of one inch, then reheat the piece in the forge.

Next, work the edges of your piece into an octagon, then round. Finally, reheat your piece.

Step 5: Shaping the prongs

While minding that the prongs remain at the same angle from the centerline (around 30 Degrees), open your prongs to a 'Y' shape. Next, place the done Y shape piece upside down over your anvil and strike its handle's end to shape it. After completing this, reheat.

Next, bend the curve over the horn away from the centerline and bend another curve towards the centerline (the aim is to ensure that the tips are parallel, that is, about half of one inch from the centerline).

Next, place the prongs over the edge of your anvil, bend them to an angle of 15 Degrees, rotate them to 180 Degrees, and finally bend the neck to suit. By now, you should see your forged fork coming to life!

Step 6: Finishing

Reheat the fork in the forge and when you take it out, brush off the slag and the scale using the metal wire brush. Immediately after, dip the fork in a bucket of oil and finally hold it next to the forge until it turns to a matte black!

Project 4: Coil Spring Punch

For this project, you will require;

- A piece of coil spring (you can use any metal rod)

- A small forge (if you have a big one, it is fine too)

- Anvil.

- Hammer.

- Tongs.

- Angle grinder.

Step 1: Cut down the coil spring

Cut the coil spring into a comfortable size using an angle grinder (remember that they should be long enough to keep your hands safe from getting burned), then heat it in your forge.

Step 2: Tape the piece

Use your hummer to taper the end of the heated piece into a point (remember to make the point flat). Next, round off the edges of the taper by striking the rod repeatedly and doing so while rotating it.

Step 3: Finishing

Grind your final piece and polish if needed. You can also leave it unfinished if you want your punch to have a rough look.

Project 5: Ax

For this project, you will need:

- Forge

- Tongs

- Hammer

- Mild steel (3/8 inches thick and 2 inches wide)

- Borax

Step 1: Forge and bend the piece of mild steel

For this step, ensure your forge is at a temperature of 1,200 degrees Celsius. Once heated enough, take it off the forge and start bending it while ensuring the ends are even. Before closing the ends, insert a carbon steel slab and add borax between the layers. This trick is important because it will add quality to your ax.

After the ends get closed down, put your piece back in the forge and heat it again (maintain the temperature). Take it off the forge, add borax, and hammer the layers together. You will do this process severally to force each layer to become one.

Step 2: Weld

As you hammer, the eye created may seem out of shape, which is okay. The next step will be to do some welding with a drift. The welding should be done to the steel closest to the eye to avoid breaking, and once done, hammer out the shape of the ax head. Leave the eye drift as it is because it will help hold the shape intact.

Step 3: Shape your ax

This step will require you to reheat your piece severally. Start smoothing and thinning the edge of your blade as soon as you finish welding and shaping out the shape of the ax.

To harden your ax, heat the edged side of your ax, ensuring it heats up to 800 degrees and that the ax heats slowly while you turn and flip it after every few minutes.

Step 4: Quench and temper your ax

Remove the ax from the forge, and dip it in a bucket full of water to harden the steel of the ax—finally, sand down the ax to achieve a clean and smooth look. Remember to sharpen the ax and fit it in the handle.

Now that the blade is ready, it is time to make the handle. To do this, follow the following steps:

- **Step 1:** Get your freshly cut piece of yellow birch, hophornbeam, or sugar maple. The wood you choose must be green, straight-grained, and free of knots. It should also be 10 to 16 inches in diameter. The next step is to split it into billets.

- **Step 2:** Spilt the bolt you have chosen to billets. Next, either split out or hew and score the triangle inside the billet and work on removing the bark. Ensure the billet is one-half inches thick and four inches wide. You have a lot of choices to make; 19 to 22 inches for axes set for shaping, 20 to 26 inches for camping axes, and 28 to 31 inches for splitting and chopping axes.

- **<u>Step 3</u>:** Score and hew the handle into rough shape, ensuring you stick to your pattern. That area that fits into the eye of the ax head should be an oversized rectangle of the wood, and you should make the shaft to a measurement ratio of one to two (that is, thickness to width). Next, dry the handle for a few weeks.

On matters drying, keep both ends of the handle sealed to prevent drying faster. You can mix white glue and hot water, then smear the mixture on the end grain of the handle. After it's dry, sand, scrap (with a broken glass), and smoothen it with a spokeshave. Last but not least, treat your handle with a coat or two of boiled linseed oil and thin it with turpentine.

- **<u>Step 4</u>:** Take the ax and hang it on your dried angle. Next, tap off the squared-off part of the fawn's foot until it perfectly pulls the ax head onto the handle. After fixing the wooden wedge in place, apply a wood-swelling fluid. Use products such as Chair-Loc or Wonderlok'Em Tite Chairs because they are perfect at swelling and solidifying the wood.

Project 6: Spoon

For this project, you will require;

- Ball peen hammer

- Forge

- Flat-faced hammer

- Anvil

- Tongs

- Vise

- Metal wire brush

- Steel Stock

Step 1: Upset the steel stock

Hold the steel stock at the far edge of your anvil and hammer it to taper. Next, place it in the forge but note that you should only heat one-half of the steel. Once the metal is hot, remove it from the forge and quench it.

While holding your hot part of the stock with a pair of tongs on the anvil, strike the cold end of the piece until it bends or until it cools to red. Next, straighten and flatten it while rolling it over and over, then reheat it in the forge (you should do all this while upsetting the piece of stock with hard hammer blows).

Hold the piece from one end and straighten it. Only the curve (with its high side facing up) should be on the anvil. Then, strike the high spot until the piece is three-quarter inches at the widest part.

Step 2: Draw out your metal

The next step should be rolling the piece over to shape the edges into an octagon. Using a round face hammer and anvil horn, strike the piece until the neck reduces to $3/8$ inches at the thinnest part of the piece.

Step 3: Shape the handle

Take back the piece in the forge and flatten it in the middle (stop only when both sides are a quarter-inch thick). Next, blow the piece to spread the edges to shape the handle. Remember that each time you strike the face of the piece, rotate it so that the anvil is under the blow. The aim is to thin the piece to 3/16 of one inch and shape it into what you desire.

Next, clean the piece's faces using your flat-faced hammer, then reheat the piece. Take it out and spread the edge of the handle (the blows should be consistent and overlapping. Also, ensure you flatten it to $3/8$ of one inch). Work any high spots while minding the thin edge and rotating the contact.

Step 4: Shape the neck and the bowl

Through constant and overlapping blows, work on flattening and shaping your piece until the size is not more than an eighth of an inch. Next, place the flat section over the hardy wall and use the ball-peen hammer to sink it to a depth of $1/3$ to $1/8$ of an inch. Strike the two points of contact.

Next, deal with the edge and back of the spoon (use the ball anvil in the vise). Next, make an offset bend in the neck of the spoon and place it over the edge of the anvil in a concave-down position.

Next, strike the materials of the anvil (aim for a small bend). Finally, rotate the piece to 180 degrees and strike the material of the spoon until your spoon sits well —do this while the piece is perpendicular to the paper)

Step 5: Finish up

After reheating your piece, scrape off the scale and the slag with a metal wire brush, dip it in a bucket of oil, and if you like, hold it next to the forge until it turns matte black.

Project 7: Iron Triangle Dinner Bell

For this project, you will need:

- Pliers

- Chop Saw

- Screws

- Metal Bender

- Length of Cording/Chain

- Bracket

- Rounds of Metal Iron Rods

Forging Made Easy

Step 1:

Use your chop saw to cut two pieces of iron rods, one for the bell and the other for the mallet. Next, place the rod into your metal bender and rotate it to shape it. You are free to rotate it as much as you want since it depends on your design. However, most dinner bells have triangular shapes with 60-degree curves.

Step 2:

Reposition the iron by pulling the crank handle back. Next, curve one end of a length of iron into the shape you want (you can try making an angle or a circular top —the bottom line is that it should be a shape you can easily and comfortably grasp).

Step 3:

Attach a bracket to where you want to hang the bell. Finally, attach the bell and mallet to your bracket using the cording or chain.

Project 8: Bottle Opener

For this project, you will need;

- Scrap Round Bar

- Copper wire

- Mini files

- Vise grips

- Gloves

- Anvil

- Metal Wire Brush (Normal and Brass)

- A Dremel attached with a grinder

- Tongs

- Hammer

- Welder

- Safety glasses

- Propane torch

Step 1: Square the iron

After getting the metal out of the forge, hit the scrap metal two or three times with your hammer. Remember to do this while the hammer's face is parallel to the anvil's surface.

Next, rotate the metal at an angle of 90 degrees and redo the heating. Do the hitting in a way that allows you to work your way down the length of your bar while also managing to check for squareness. The bar should also be straight. Also, remember to brush off the scale each time you heat the bar to avoid the scale from embedding in the metal during the hammering process.

Step 2: Form the '8'

After heating the metal, hold the tip of the bar over the edge of your anvil and hammer it down carefully. Next, gradually slide the metal off the edge of the anvil while simultaneously keeping the hammering aimed at one spot (you will notice the curve starting to form).

To ensure your curve is uniform, have the end of your bar meet the middle of the bar.

When you notice the curve forming, free-form the rest of the loop by hitting your bar from different angles —the secret is to reheat the bar and work it in different ways until the 8 forms.

Step 3: Forming the Hook

Using your hammer, strike the bar heavily to flatten it but be keen to have the surface even. After straightening the bar fully as desired, give one end of the bar a slight taper. Next, create a small hook as you made the 8 but ensure it fits well around the bottle caps.

Next, make a larger hook that should face the opposite end of the bar (this hook will loop over the base of the 8). Be sure to have the hook's size large enough to wrap the base of your 8 completely.

Step 4: Attach the two parts

Join the two sections of the bottle opener by first heating up the hook. Next, drop the hot hook into place and hammer its end down. Next, hammer the opener until it sits flat but be careful not to bend the opener hook or the 8.

Step 5: Finish up

Use the Dremel grinder and mini files to grind the slag caused by the welding off. Finish the bottle opener with a thin brass coating or any coating of your choice (use a propane torch to heat the bottle opener because the forge can easily burn the brass).

Next, clamp the bottle opener in the vise, pass the propane torch's blue flame over the opener for 30 seconds and scrub it with the brass brush for another minute or so. Once satisfied, quench it in a half bucket of water and repeat the process with the other half of the bottle opener.

Project 9: 20-Inch Meat Skewers

For this project, you will need;

- 3/16-inch Square Stock

- Bolt Cutters

- Propane Torch

- Anvil

- Hammer (Flat and Round)

- Tongs

- Vise

Step 1: Work on the rat's tail of the meat skewer

Light your propane torch and hit the tip of the rod only. Heat about an inch of the material and strike it with the hammer until it becomes thin and not very sharp taper.

Next, reheat the same tip, take a smaller hammer and make a rat's tail. Place the rod on the anvil and at the edge, curl it down, flip it over, and flip it back to yourself.

Step 2: Make the bends

Heat everything else behind the rat's tail you made in step one (heat about four inches). Put the heated metal in your jig attached in your vice, and go all the way until it bends (bend it until it almost touches the rat's tail). Next, hit the joint where the rod meets the rat's tail and bend it back.

Step 3: Work on the twist

Depending on how big you want your skewer to be, cut it first before moving on to putting the rod in the forge or before heating it with the torch. Then as we did in step one, heat the tip and hit it with the hammer. Lock the rat's tail in the vice, and with a twisting tool or pliers, twist the rod (do not twist too fast; give it time to bend. Also, do multiple twists). If one part gets tighter, re-set the rod by pushing the length closer to the vice.

Step 4: Finishing

Heat the rods and rub with coconut oil.

Project 10: Steel Dice

For this project, you will need;

- One-inch square stock (get one that you can easily cut into a dice)

- Electric shears

- Tongs

- Anvil

- Forge

- Punch

- Hammer

- Belt sander

Step 1: Cut the dice

Cut the stock at one inch using your electric shears.

Step 2: Make the pips

Use a punch to dot the pips, then put your dice in the forge. When you take them out of the forge with your tongs, use your punch to make the holes deeper.

Step 3:

Grind the edges using your belt sander, and that's it: easy-peasy!

Project 11: Drill Bit for Wood Pegs.

For this project, you will need:

- Round bar

- Anvil

- Forge

- Hammer

- Tongs

- Punch

- Vise

- Metal flux powder

Step 1: Forge the eye

Put the bar in the forge. After it has heated up, bend out the eye. From the tip, strike it down and offset the central position.

Step 2: Forge the scarf

Forge a little bit of a scarf by thinning down one end while cutting it off. Take the remainder of the part you cut off and fold it past the place you thinned out. Ensure the transition is thin enough to blend in with the parent bar properly.

As you keep hitting it, ensure you use your metal brush to keep it is as clean as possible. The aim is to get some flux and close the tip-up to touch the metal bar. If the hole where you will put the handle does not form as needed, reheat the metal bar, add some flux powder and strike again.

To ensure the eye of the drill is round, try fitting the biggest size of punch in the eye, which will help have the piece of round wood fit in the drill bit hole.

Step 3: Make the trident fork

Heat the end of the bar, and at the tip, cut the square across and make a trident fork. Heat the trident forks and flatten the three forks, flatten the two sides of the fork and straighten the middle part of the fork.

Step 4: Twist the middle spike

After reheating the stock, use a vice to hold the bar and a pair of tongs to twist the spike. For one of the two remaining spikes of the trident, use the edge of the anvil and bend it.

Step 5: Make twists

Hold the end part of the bar with a vise, and with the help of a metal bar, hit it down to push that section of the trident lower than the one we twisted in the previous step. Using the bigger part of tongs, push the metal bar a few inches from the vise grip, and twist the bar. For the twisting to become easier to do, keep reheating the stock.

Step 6: Finishing up

Use a grinder to smoothen out the sides of the drill and file the tip of the drill. Also, use a metal brush to remove the slag, and that's it!

Project 12: Splinter EDC Knife

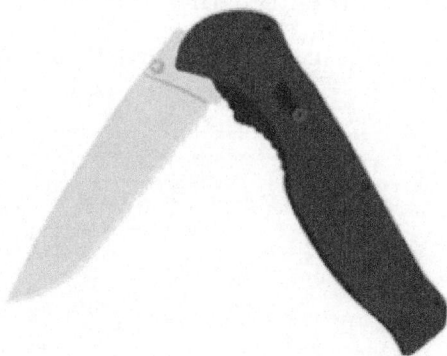

For this project, you will need;

- A mosaic Damascus stock

- Grinder

- Tin snips

- Forge

- Tongs

- Sand Paper

- Bog oak

- Epoxy glue

Step 1: Get your knife skeleton

Cut out a rectangle with the Damascus knife as reference (it will help you know the size), then mill it down with your snips to get the pattern. To be more accurate, trace the Damascus knife, put the traced paper on the already cut piece of Damascus steel, and further cut the piece to have the parent design.

Step 2: Drill holes.

With the skeleton made, it is time to drill holes into it. Put the skeleton in the forge and drill in the holes. With the help of a small drill, scribe the bevel of your skeleton. Next, use your grinder to sharpen your blade. Take the knife back to the forge and then treat it in oil.

Step 3: Finish up on the blade

Take the knife back to the forge and after it is hot enough, let it cool down and grind the blade to sharpen it. Next, hand sand the whole blade, then treat it by dipping it in oil. Next, etch the blade in ferric chloride (it helps enhance the visual aesthetic of the blade).

Step 4: Work on the handle

Use a bog oak to make the blade handle. After cutting the bog oak to the size of your handle (you should have two pieces of wood), re-treat the blade, then drill three holes on the blade's handle. Take the handle of your blade and drill holes in them (ensure the woods fit the handle).

After fitting in the handle pegs and attaching the wood to the metal using epoxy, sand the handle to give it that smooth look, then sharpen the blade.

One more thing, while working on the blade, you can decide to etch in a signature mark to have the blade unique and customized.

Project 13: Infinity Cube

For this project, you will need:

- 16-millimeter square metal stock

- Professional Primer Spray Paint

- Chisel

- Hammer

Step 1: Color and mark your stock

You can color it using any color you like. Next, follow the next pattern to mark the bends you will make. One short piece, two long pieces, and one short piece. Mark out the bends using a chisel and hammer.

Step 2: Make the bends

Right from the edge, make your overlaps by putting the stock in the forge and bending the stock right at the marks you made in step one. As you make the bends, ensure to clean them with the metal brush to remove the slag. Let it cool, then use a hammer to straighten the metal bar.

Step 3: Bend your stock

With a propane torch, heat the bends and curve the bar. Ensure that when you make one bend, you allow the bar to cool before you move on to the next because the bar tends to be quite soft. To hold the bar while doing the bends, you can use the vise.

You will make mistakes here and there while trying to get the shape; use the picture on this project as a guide.

Step 4: Finishing up

Once done, you will notice that you have two ends that need joining. You can do this in many ways; one of my favorites is heating the tips with a propane torch, making a hole with a punch, and putting a peg. After the peg is through, heat the joint you have made and strike it until it sticks together.

Finally, spray the cube, and you are good to go!

Project 14: Fire Pit

For this project, you will need:

- 55-gallon drum

- Black masking tape

- Hand sander

- Electric cutter

- Acetone metal cleaner

- High-temperature grill spray paints

- Half-inch drill

- Wire wheel

- Belt sander

- Hammer

- Anvil

- Hand press machine

- Aluminum pop rivets

- Tin Snips

- Forge

Step 1: Mark the drum half vertically

To do this, mark it off with tape because we need to grind the bottom half part of the drum. Next, with a hand sander, sand the half section of the drum (the top part). To prevent the drum from rusting, you can spray the sanded part.

Step 2: Cut the drum in half

Mark the top-half part at the mid-section, flip it over, and do the same on the other sides of the sanded part of the drum. Next, cut it in half, then sand it.

Step 3: Clean and spray the drum

Clean the surface of the half part of your metal with acetone. Next, spray the drum (ensure the sprays are high-temperature grill spray paints). As the paint is drying off, move on to the next step.

Step 4: Make windows on lid number 2

Take the other lid and measure it to make windows on its top. After marking the windows, cut them and put in a screen underneath for the lid. You can do this using a grinder. Next, drill each of the corners of the windows with a half-inch drill to get nice clean radiuses. Next, cut off the windows.

Step 5: Work on the tabs: Smoothen the tabs

Grind off the sharp edges made by the cutting, then sand off the remaining part of the drum. Next, use the lid you cut off to make tabs of the lid (this supports the lid when you put it on top so that it does not just fall off). Grind the edges to smoothen and flatten the lid, then use a bandsaw to cut each tab.

Step 6: Work on the tab: straighten the tab and drill holes

Using your hammer and anvil, hit on the lid to flatten it. Next, sander it to eliminate the color previously on the lid. Next, mark and drill holes. You will use these holes to attach the lid to the already half-cut top with holes. Remember to mark a line down the middle, which you will later bend so that when fitted on the main lid, it will have that inner edge of the bottom of the pit.

Step 7: Attach the tabs to the pit.

After cutting down the tabs from the cut-out lids, use your belt sander to grind their edges. Next, using aluminum pop rivets and the hand press machine, attach the tabs to the pit.

Step 8: Cut out your lathe and fit it on the pit

Take your metal lathe mesh (this will act as the screen for the top of the fire pit), mark it according to your pit's size using your tin snips. You will attach this lathe to your pit using pop rivets that will hold it together.

Step 9: Work on the legs of the pit

Take a steel bar stock and put it in a forge. After it's heated, use your anvil to curve one tip inwards. With this, you will have a curved stand. Make four of these stands. To can make the stands smoother and more admirable by grinding the edges with your belt sander.

Step 10: Put holes in your pit 'feet'

Put the stock back in the forge and punch two holes in them. The holes should be as big as your intended screws. If the punch fails to give you that result, you can use a drill.

Step 11: Attach the feet to the pit

Using a drill, use the holes you made to the feet of the pit and make holes to the pit. Next, put screws to attach the feet to the pit.

Step 12: Make the pit handle

Using another piece of the tabs we took out earlier, make a handle out of them. Depending on the measurements of the handle you want to have, you will need to drill the holes first, cut as much as you can with a bandsaw, and grind the edges with a grinder.

After the handle is set, which is flat at the moment, clamp it in the vise and begin rounding it over. The best way to do this is to clamp the metal together with a huge cold chisel in the vise. This will make the rounding easier. To complete the rounding, you can do it with your hand.

At the end of the rounded part, bend down the flattened sides with your hand and use the vise to bend the base (where the drilled holes are). Go back to the top half of the pit and in the middle, drill holes, and attach the handle to the pit using rivets.

Step 13: Work on the bottom of the grill

Using some of the tabs left, cut out some small rectangle, put it on a vise, and bend it. We will use them as the steel base for the grill.

Use a 16-gauge piece of steel and cut out two pieces. These two pieces of steel should have drainage holes. Next, go to the bottom part of the pit and drill holes where you will attach the gaps we made earlier on this step. Finally, paint the pit.

Put on your firewood, and you are ready to enjoy the outdoors!

Project 15: Rose

For this project, you will need:

- Steel stock

- Forge

- Bandsaw

- Cut hardy

- Anvil

- Hammer

Step 1: Mark out the rose

Mark the steel bar. Start marking out where you will be cutting with a bandsaw (this will be the stem of the rose). For the petals, mark equally (you can choose the measurements, just make sure they are not big since we need the petals to be visible).

Step 2: Work on striking down the petals

After cutting the metal stem and making the petal marks using a saw, put the stock in the forge. Next, use the hammer to strike the pieces on the anvil. Remember to use the horn of the anvil to spread them down.

Be careful not to hammer down the area close to the joints because it might damage the shape of the rose. Reheat each petal after striking. Also, hit the stem to be as thin as possible.

Step 3: Texture the petals

After having the stem and the paddles forged out, put the rose in the forge and begin texturing it with the cross-peen hammer. As you hack the stock, do not hack in between the petals.

Step 4: Fold the petals

Knock the stem down with a 90-degree angle bend. Just remember that the stem will be on the outside of the rose. Using your tongs, hold the last petal and strike the stem — this will avoid any unnecessary stress to the petals.

After reheating the stock, use the end of the anvil and hammer to strike into a curve the first petal from the stem and work on getting a tighter fold. Next, reheat and do the same curving on the second leaf and so on until you get to the final leaf.

Step 6: Finishing up

Use the hold on your anvil and tongs to put the stem in the hole and push in the rose bulb. The aim is to spread the petals so that the rose can be more realistic. If the anvil hole does not give you the intended results, you can grip the stem with a vise and do the same.

Project 16: Butcher's Hook

For this project, you will need:

- Hex bar mystery steel

- Anvil

- Forge

- Hammer

- Chisel

Forging Made Easy

Step 1: Forge out the eye

After taking out the bar from the forge, use a chisel to punch through the steel. You will have to flip it for the hole to be complete. Remember, you are heating one end of the bar. Reheat the stock.

Put the stock upright and strike it down from the end that is not hot —this will make the hole/eye bigger. Next, use your hammer to straighten the bar out. With a punch and while eyeing the anvil hole, punch the hole further to make it rounder and bigger. Reheat and use the punch once more to enlarge the hole.

Step 2: Work to get a pointy end

Depending on the length you want for the hook, reheat the stock and cut it down. Next, take a hammer and strike the end of the bar down. Strike until the end of the bar becomes pointy.

Step 3: Form the hook

Using the end of your anvil, bend the hot metal to form a hook — you can keep reheating it if the striking becomes harder to do. Next, clean with a metal brush, and you are good to go!

Project 17: Maple Leaf Bowl

For this project, you will need:

- Anvil

- Hammer

- Flat stock

- Chisel

- Punch

- Forge

- Spring swage

- Tongs

- Rawhide mallet

Step 1: Make your center vane

After drawing out the leaf's skeleton, put it in the forge. After getting it out, put it in a center vane, then use a punch, spring swage, or chisel, work back towards the stem. You should see the same bulging center vane if you look behind your leaf. Put it back in the forge.

Step 2: Make the veins

Using the same tools you used in step one, create additional veins branching from the vein. To do it best, use your tongs to grab the side of the leaf. This way, everything will stay in line.

Step 3: Iron out the leaf and add secondary veins

Straightening is important because step 2 made it cupped. Use a cold chisel locked in a pair of tongs and a hammer to strike in the secondary veins. Remember to clean it with a metal brush, then return it to the forge. Be aware enough to avoid biting on the other veins and use the full width of your chisel. Reheat the stock.

Step 4: Work down the leaf

Use the swage block and the rawhide mallet to work it down. Remember to do very few hits on the ridges. Next, where the lobes are, bend the initial points out and give them a back curl. Reheat the stock.

Using the end of your anvil, bend out the stem on the back. You can choose to round it up or leave it as it is. Next, get the forged scale off with a metal wire brush.

Project 18: Spatula and Ladle Set

For this project, you will need;

- Spatula and ladle blanks

- Hammer

- Anvil

- Forge

- Rawhide mallet

- Vise

Step 1: Get your blanks

Cut the draws off your blanks because they are plasma cut. Use a hammer and an anvil to set it up on edge and chip the dross.

Step 2: Texture and spread the handle

Use a pair of tongs to hold the stock on its top side and start texturing it while spreading the handle. Next, reheat the handle and give the handle a cup shape by hitting it on the step of the anvil. Next, hammer the handle on the edges to get a better curve. Reheat the handle.

Step 3: Work on the handles' curvature.

Use a soft face mallet or a rawhide mallet and the anvil's horn to shape the handle (curvature). Next, clean it with a mallet. Once you get this handle done, do the same to the ladle handle.

Step 4: Work on the ends

Heat the end of the spatula and put a small taper by forging it with a little bevel. To do this, place it on the outside edge of the anvil to help you get that needed forged bevel.

Next, reheat it and bend it to ensure it does not dive into the pan —this will make handling the spatula more comfortable. Next, reheat and take it to the vise and grip it in (about three-quarters of an inch or so in) between two pieces of angle iron and bend it right over with a hammer. You can also bend the same over an anvil. Reheat and do another round of hitting.

Step 5: Dishing the ladle

To do this, equip the vise with a cupping tool (this is a pipe with a bar welded across the bottom, with edges rolled out). With the cupping tool and the ball peen hammer, sink your ladle. First, aim for the edges by hitting dead in the center of the stock (strike while moving the material around). Remember to hit on the side that will put weight on your handle.

Step 6: Finishing

To finish it off, wire the tools down, then coat them with your favorite cooking oil or food-safe oil. Do not use peanut oil because of allergies.

Project 19: Banana Hanger

For this project, you will need:

- Forge

- Anvil

- Hammer

- Vise

- Steel bar

- Punch

Step 1: Split up the legs

Heat the steel bar and cut them into two. Do not cut it all the way through; have the cut go halfway. Next, take the stock and draw down a taper on the other end.

After drawing most of the work, hammer the piece on an anvil to remove all the hammer marks. The result of this step should be a taper at one end of the bar and a split on the other end (the split ends will finally become the banana hanger legs).

Step 2: Make a bull's eye

Punch the material to create a bull's eye where the split ends, then reheat the stock. Next, using the anvil's hole, use a punch to make a drift hole. Ensure the hole is big enough because you will need to thread the large tapered end back later. Increase the size of drifts you use until the hole becomes big enough.

Step 3: Make the scroll

Use your anvil to open up the legs of the hanger. After you draw out both legs, make an asymmetrical taper but leave a little bit of mass at the end. The aim is to create a halfpenny scroll, so dress it up until completion. If making the scroll is harder, use the anvil's horn.

Step 4: Make the scrolls stand upright

Beat on the scrolls themselves to get them to twist and lay against the anvil. The aim is to have it stand perfectly upright on its own. Next, clean it all out with a metal wire brush.

Step 5: Shape the hanger

Heat the upper side of the hanger and shape it into a scroll using a hammer and the anvil's horn to help with the bending. Start by bending the end to get a hook shape, then clean it with a metal wire brush.

Next, heat and strike further and keep tucking it so that the whole piece comes right around. Next, lace it right through the hole where your tongs are. The pointy end of the bar should curve in a way that it gets right into the bull's eye we made earlier.

Next, heat the end of the hook and bend it backward on your anvil horn (this will make the upwards looking curve where you will be resting your bananas. Finally, clean your hanger and paint it.

Conclusion

Black and bladesmithing are fun, and whether you are doing it as a hobby or as a career, you have endless projects to create.

From these 25 projects, I am sure you can find one or two to try out. With the help of this guide, I hope that you will soon be in the history books for creating masterpieces that take the world by storm!

You should note that maintenance is quite critical.

As we have seen in this book, black and bladesmithing involve a lot of tools made of metals. These metals and any other tools require frequent cleaning. You have the option of keeping a clean rug and soaking it in some tung oil.

Good luck!

PS: I'd like your feedback. If you are happy with this book, please leave a review on Amazon.

Please leave a review for this book on Amazon by visiting the page below:

https://amzn.to/2VMR5qr

Printed in Great Britain
by Amazon

43793120R00076